BIRDING VIEWING AREAS

Western Coastal waters offer some of the richest and most productive habitats for the world's seabirds. From the Gulf of California and its islands that serve as breeding grounds for much of the world's population of Heermann's gull, royal tern, and brown pelican; to San Francisco Bay, a stopover point for roughly a million migratory birds on their Pacific Flyway journey; to the Alaskan/Fjordland Pacific where a large proportion of the world's populations of Cassin's auklet and ancient murrelets reside, the Western Coastal region is home to a multitude of unique birds.

1. Alaska Maritime National Wildlife Refuge (NWR)
2. Copper River Delta
3. Mendenhall Wetlands State Game Refuge
4. Delkatla Slough
5. Pacific Rim National Park
6. Brackendale
7. Reifel Bird Sanctuary
8. Olympic National Park
9. Gray's Harbor NWR
10. Nisqually NWR Complex
11. Cape Meares NWR
12. Yaquina Head Outstanding Natural Area
13. Bandon Marsh NWR
14. Humboldt Bay NWR
15. Point Reyes National Seashore
16. San Francisco Bay NWR
17. Monterey Bay National Marine Sanctuary
18. Channel Islands National Park
19. Newport Bay
20. Tijuana Slough NWR

Waterford Press publishes reference guides that introduce readers to nature observation, outdoor recreation and survival skills. Product information is featured on the website: www.waterfordpress.com.

Text & illustrations © 2022 Waterford Press Inc. All rights reserved. Photos © Shutterstock. To order or for information on custom published products please call 800-434-2555 or email orderdesk@waterfordpress.com. For permissions or to share comments email editor@waterfordpress.com.

Made in the USA

ISBN 978-1-62005-552-6 $7.95 U.S.

WESTERN COASTAL BIRDS

WESTERN COASTAL BIRDS – A Waterproof Folding Guide to Familiar Species

Kavanagh/Leung

A Waterproof Folding Guide to Familiar Species

WATERBIRDS

Red-throated Loon
Gavia stellata To 25 in. (63 cm)

Arctic Loon
Gavia arctica To 26 in. (65 cm)
Note white flank patch.

Pacific Loon
Gavia pacifica To 25 in. (63 cm)

Winter

Summer

Common Loon
Gavia immer To 3 ft. (90 cm)
Has a black and white checkered back.

Horned Grebe
Podiceps auritus To 15 in. (38 cm)
Note reddish neck and ear tufts.

Pied-billed Grebe
Podilymbus podiceps
To 13 in. (33 cm)
Note banded white bill.

Eared Grebe
Podiceps nigricollis To 14 in. (35 cm)
Note black neck and golden ear tufts.

Western Grebe
Aechmophorus occidentalis
To 25 in. (63 cm)
Has a two-note call.

Clark's Grebe
Aechmophorus clarkii
To 25 in. (63 cm)
Has a one-note call.

Red-necked Grebe
Podiceps grisegena To 19 in. (48 cm)

Tundra Swan
Cygnus columbianus To 4.5 ft. (1.4 m)
Note yellow mark on black bill.

Trumpeter Swan
Cygnus buccinator To 6 ft. (1.8 m)
Note stout black bill.

WATERBIRDS

Snow Goose
Chen caerulescens
To 38 in. (95 cm)
Wing tips are black.

Brant
Branta bernicla
To 26 in. (65 cm)
Note white neck mark.

Canada Goose
Branta canadensis
To 43 in. (1.1 m)

Emperor Goose
Chen canagica
To 28 in. (70 cm)

Greater White-fronted Goose
Anser albifrons
To 30 in. (75 cm)

Gadwall
Mareca strepera To 23 in. (58 cm)

Mallard
Anas platyrhynchos To 28 in. (70 cm)

Green-winged Teal
Anas crecca
To 16 in. (40 cm)

Blue-winged Teal
Spatula discors
To 16 in. (40 cm)
Male has a white facial crescent.

Long-tailed Duck
Clangula hyemalis To 22 in. (55 cm)

American Wigeon
Mareca americana To 23 in. (58 cm)

Cinnamon Teal
Spatula cyanoptera To 17 in. (43 cm)

WATERBIRDS

Redhead
Aythya americana To 22 in. (55 cm)

Northern Shoveler
Spatula clypeata To 20 in. (50 cm)
Named for its large spatulate bill.

Canvasback
Aythya valisineria To 2 ft. (60 cm)
Note sloping forehead and black bill.

Common Goldeneye
Bucephala clangula To 20 in. (50 cm)
Male has a white facial spot.

Ring-necked Duck
Aythya collaris To 18 in. (45 cm)
Note white ring near bill tip.

Barrow's Goldeneye
Bucephala islandica To 20 in. (50 cm)
Male has a white facial crescent.

Bufflehead
Bucephala albeola To 15 in. (38 cm)

Harlequin Duck
Histrionicus histrionicus
To 17 in. (43 cm)

Wood Duck
Aix sponsa To 20 in. (50 cm)

Northern Pintail
Anas acuta To 30 in. (75 cm)

Lesser Scaup
Aythya affinis To 18 in. (45 cm)
Note peaked crown.

Greater Scaup
Aythya marila To 20 in. (50 cm)
Note rounded head.

WATERBIRDS

Common Eider
Somateria mollissima To 28 in. (70 cm)

King Eider
Somateria spectabilis
To 2 ft. (60 cm)

Ruddy Duck
Oxyura jamaicensis
To 16 in. (40 cm)
Note cocked tail.

White-winged Scoter
Melanitta fusca To 23 in. (58 cm)
Note white wing patches.

Surf Scoter
Melanitta perspicillata To 20 in. (50 cm)
Note white patches on nape and forehead of male.

Black Scoter
Melanitta americana To 20 in. (50 cm)

American Coot
Fulica americana
To 16 in. (40 cm)

Hooded Merganser
Lophodytes cucullatus To 20 in. (50 cm)
Note white head crest and thin bill.

Common Gallinule
Gallinula galeata
To 14 in. (35 cm)

Common Merganser
Mergus merganser To 27 in. (68 cm)

Sora
Porzana carolina
To 10 in. (25 cm)
Note stubby yellow bill and black patch on face and throat.

Red-breasted Merganser
Mergus serrator To 27 in. (68 cm)
Note thin bill and prominent head crest.

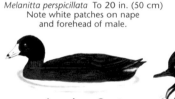

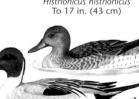

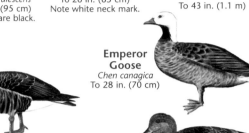

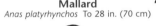

Solitary Sandpiper
Tringa solitaria
To 9 in. (23 cm)

Spotted Sandpiper
Actitis macularius
To 8 in. (20 cm)
Breast is spotted.

Least Sandpiper
Calidris minutilla
To 6 in. (15 cm)

Western Sandpiper
Calidris mauri
To 7 in. (18 cm)

Semipalmated Sandpiper
Calidris pusilla
To 7 in. (18 cm)

Long-billed Curlew
Numenius americanus
To 26 in. (65 cm)
Long bill is slightly downturned.

Marbled Godwit
Limosa fedoa
To 20 in. (50 cm)
Long bill is slightly upturned.

Ruddy Turnstone
Arenaria interpres
To 10 in. (25 cm)

Black Turnstone
Arenaria melanocephala
To 9 in. (23 cm)

Surfbird
Aphriza virgata
To 8 in. (20 cm)
Common along coastlines in winter.

Long-billed Dowitcher
Limnodromus scolopaceus
To 12 in. (30 cm)
Breeding male has a rusty breast.

Short-billed Dowitcher
Limnodromus griseus
To 12 in. (30 cm)
Feeds in a 'sewing machine' fashion while probing for food.

Dunlin
Calidris alpina
To 9 in. (23 cm)
Note black belly patch.

Sanderling
Calidris alba To 8 in. (20 cm)
Runs in and out with waves along shorelines.

Red Knot
Calidris canutus
To 12 in. (30 cm)
Plump, red-breasted shorebird.

Willet
Tringa semipalmata
To 17 in. (43 cm)
Wings flash black-and-white in flight.

Lesser Yellowlegs
Tringa flavipes
To 10 in. (25 cm)
Call is a 1-3 note whistle.

Greater Yellowlegs
Tringa melanoleuca
To 15 in. (38 cm)
Call is a 3-5 note whistle.

Killdeer
Charadrius vociferus
To 12 in. (30 cm)
Note two breast bands.

Whimbrel
Numenius phaeopus
To 20 in. (50 cm)
Note long decurved bill and striped crown.

American Golden-Plover
Pluvialis dominica
To 12 in. (30 cm)
Mantle is gold-spotted.

Semipalmated Plover
Charadrius semipalmatus
To 8 in. (20 cm)
Note single breast band.

Snowy Plover
Charadrius alexandrinus
To 6 in. (15 cm)

Black-bellied Plover
Pluvialis squatarola
To 14 in. (35 cm)

Black Oystercatcher
Haematopus bachmani
To 18 in. (45 cm)

Red-necked Phalarope
Phalaropus lobatus
To 8 in. (20 cm)
Female is more colorful than the male.

Black-necked Stilt
Himantopus mexicanus
To 17 in. (43 cm)

American Avocet
Recurvirostra americana
To 20 in. (50 cm)

Virginia Rail
Rallus limicola
To 9 in. (23 cm)
Rusty bird has a gray face and barred flanks.

Clapper Rail
Rallus longirostris
To 16 in. (40 cm)
Note barred flanks and upturned tail.

Wandering Tattler
Tringa incana
To 12 in. (30 cm)
Note barred underparts.

Wilson's Snipe
Gallinago delicata
To 12 in. (30 cm)

Cattle Egret
Bubulcus ibis
To 20 in. (50 cm)

Snowy Egret
Egretta thula
To 26 in. (65 cm)
Note black bill and yellow feet.

American Bittern
Botaurus lentiginosus
To 23 in. (58 cm)

Sandhill Crane
Antigone canadensis
To 4 ft. (1.2 m)

Green Heron
Butorides virescens
To 22 in. (55 cm)

Great Egret
Ardea alba
To 38 in. (95 cm)
Note yellow bill and black feet.

White-faced Ibis
Plegadis chihi
To 2 ft. (60 cm)

Great Blue Heron
Ardea herodias
To 4.5 ft. (1.4 m)

Yellow-crowned Night-Heron
Nyctanassa violacea
To 28 in. (70 cm)

Black-crowned Night-Heron
Nycticorax nycticorax
To 28 in. (70 cm)

Brown Pelican
Pelecanus occidentalis
To 50 in. (1.3 m)

American White Pelican
Pelecanus erythrorhynchos
To 5 ft. (1.5 m)

Parasitic Jaeger
Stercorarius parasiticus
To 18 in. (45 cm)
Often seen harassing terns and gulls.

Double-crested Cormorant
Phalacrocorax auritus
To 3 ft. (90 cm)
Note orange-yellow throat patch.

Pelagic Cormorant
Phalacrocorax pelagicus
To 30 in. (75 cm)
Note red throat and face.

Brandt's Cormorant
Phalacrocorax penicillatus
To 3 ft. (90 cm)
Note yellow and blue face patches.

Horned Puffin
Fratercula corniculata
To 14 in. (35 cm)

Tufted Puffin
Fratercula cirrhata
To 16 in. (40 cm)

Marbled Murrelet
Brachyramphus marmoratus
To 10 in. (25 cm)

Parakeet Auklet
Aethia psittacula
To 10 in. (25 cm)
Note stubby red bill.

Rhinoceros Auklet
Cerorhinca monocerata
To 15 in. (38 cm)
Note upturned facial plumes.

Sooty Shearwater
Puffinus griseus
To 18 in. (45 cm)

Black Skimmer
Rynchops niger
To 20 in. (50 cm)
Feeds by skimming over water with its lower bill cutting the water's surface.

Common Murre
Uria aalge
To 17 in. (43 cm)

Black-footed Albatross
Phoebastria nigripes
To 3 ft. (90 cm)
Dark seabird has light markings on its face.

Leach's Storm-Petrel
Oceanodroma leucorhoa
To 8 in. (20 cm)
Has white rump and light bars on upperwings.

Pigeon Guillemot
Cepphus columba
To 14 in. (35 cm)

Ring-billed Gull
Larus delawarensis
To 20 in. (50 cm)
Bill has dark ring.

California Gull
Larus californicus
To 23 in. (58 cm)
Note black and red spots on its bill.

Glaucous-winged Gull
Larus glaucescens
To 27 in. (68 cm)
Gray wings lack black markings. Legs are pinkish.

Black-legged Kittiwake
Rissa tridactyla
To 18 in. (45 cm)
Note black legs.

Herring Gull
Larus argentatus
To 26 in. (65 cm)
Wing tips are black with white spots. Legs are pinkish.

Western Gull
Larus occidentalis
To 27 in. (68 cm)
Large gull has a dark back.

Bonaparte's Gull
Larus philadelphia
To 14 in. (35 cm)
Small, black-headed gull.

Heermann's Gull
Larus heermanni
To 22 in. (55 cm)
Note red bill and dark tail.

Mew Gull
Larus canus
To 18 in. (45 cm)
Note smallish, unmarked yellow bill.

Arctic Tern
Sterna paradisaea
To 18 in. (45 cm)
Red-orange bill lacks a black tip.

Caspian Tern
Sterna caspia
To 2 ft. (60 cm)

Common Tern
Sterna hirundo
To 15 in. (38 cm)
Note black cap and forked tail. Orange bill is black-tipped.

Least Tern
Sternula antillarum
To 10 in. (25 cm)
Note small size and yellow bill.

Black Tern
Chlidonias niger
To 10 in. (25 cm)
Head and belly are black.

Forster's Tern
Sterna forsteri
To 15 in. (38 cm)
Note forked tail and white wing tips.

Turkey Vulture
Cathartes aura
To 32 in. (80 cm)
Note red head.

American Kestrel
Falco sparverius
To 12 in. (30 cm)

Osprey
Pandion haliaetus
To 2 ft. (60 cm)

Red-tailed Hawk
Buteo jamaicensis
To 25 in. (63 cm)
Note bright rufous tail.

Northern Harrier
Circus hudsonius
To 22 in. (55 cm)
Hunts in marshes.

Bald Eagle
Haliaeetus leucocephalus
To 40 in. (1 m)

Common Raven
Corvus corax
To 27 in. (68 cm)
Call is a hoarse croak.

American Crow
Corvus brachyrhynchos
To 22 in. (55 cm)
Call is a distinct – caw.

Northwestern Crow
Corvus caurinus
To 17 in. (43 cm)
Call is a hoarse – caw.

Red-winged Blackbird
Agelaius phoeniceus
To 9 in. (23 cm)

Belted Kingfisher
Megaceryle alcyon
To 14 in. (35 cm)

House Sparrow
Passer domesticus
To 6 in. (15 cm)

Great-tailed Grackle
Quiscalus mexicanus
To 18 in. (45 cm)
Long tail is keel-shaped.

Rock Pigeon
Columba livia
To 13 in. (33 cm)